The Leadership Nexus

Tom Desch
Beverly Bradstock

FORWARD

The Leadership Nexus is a different approach to leadership that examines how thought time is related to action. Representing an innovative way for leaders to re-align themselves and their teams, **The Leadership Nexus** helps individuals function at their highest levels of expertise and ensure that work is getting done at the right level, by the right people, at the right time.

The concept behind **The Leadership Nexus** evolved through the coaching experiences of Tom Desch and Beverly Bradstock as they have worked with numerous executives and organizations. **The Leadership Nexus** grows out of two basic principles: how a leader's thoughts and actions align is crucial for success; and, the thoughts and actions necessary for success at one level of an organization are functionally different from those at other levels.

Through this book and the accompanying Leadership Nexus Assessment, you will learn more about your leadership style, the alignment of your thoughts and actions, and how these all relate to the role you are currently inhabiting.

CONTENTS

Chapter 4

Chapter 5

Chapter 6

Chapter 7

Chapter 8

Chapter 9

Chapter 10

PREFACE

Nexus noun
nex·us | 'nek-səs
plural nexuses | 'nek-sə-səz | *or* nexus | 'nek-səs, -süs
　　1. connection, link
　　2. a connected group or series
Merriam-Webster Dictionary

Over the past couple of decades, Beverly and I, along with our team of exceptional coaches at Associates For Professional Development (AFPD), have had the honor of coaching hundreds of wonderful, challenging, dedicated, and always stimulating individuals. In our work with these talented people, who represented every level of the organizations in which they worked, we learned how to listen with our hearts as well as our ears; to step back as well as to push; and to question as well as to suggest.

As coaches, we have always tried to remain grounded in the practical realities of the worlds in which our candidates function, and to appreciate the struggles they experience as they work to become the best versions of themselves. It was in our conversations following many of these coaching sessions that we came to recognize the patterns of leadership that are put forth in **The Leadership Nexus** and the assessment that underpins it.

Experiencing the power of the interplay between thought and action and striving to better understand how their alignment creates opportunities for stronger, more effective leadership, has been a constant stimulus for us. It has led us to be better coaches and provided us with a language that better enables us talk with leaders about their skills, especially as they respond to the positional needs of their organizations.

Our hope in writing this book is that we can encourage additional conversations around the concept of leadership and bring a different perspective to our collective understanding of what it means to be a great leader.

Thomas Desch

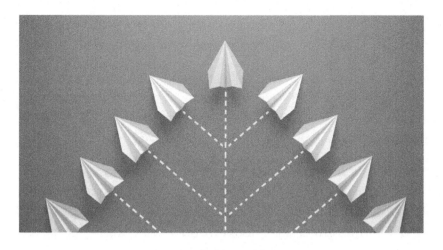

CHAPTER 1

Introduction

"Leadership, Jefferson was learning, meant knowing how to distill complexity into a comprehensible message to reach the hearts as well as the minds of the larger world."

(Observation on leadership from Jon Meacham's book:
Thomas Jefferson, The Art of Power)

A few years ago, I met with a senior leader at one of our client firms. Her level of frustration was visible as she began to talk about the difficulty, she was having in getting her direct reports to focus on the issues that were critical to the long-term health of the organization. Their focus on the detail work of the department was more powerful than anything else, regardless of her directives.

As I was talking with her about what her team was doing (and not doing), her phone rang at the same time there was a knock on her door. In the flurry of activity that followed, I learned a great deal about her, her team, and the problems they were encountering.

She answered the phone, waved in the person at the door and was immediately immersed in what looked like a disaster of epic proportions. In short order she contacted her team, called a crisis meeting and asked if we could postpone our meeting.

Since all of the individuals we had just been talking about were now gathered in a small conference room next door, I asked if I could observe her team at work. She said yes, and I was invited into what can best be described as a SWAT team command center.

For the next hour, my client and her team conducted phone meetings, emailed and texted, talked with each other, and looped in additional team members. They quickly discovered the scope and depth of the problem at hand, mapped out a plan of action, spurred other team members into action, and, in fairly short order, managed their way through what looked like a major disaster.

So, what was the problem?

At one time or another during this hour-long experience, approximately 10 high-level members of the department were directly involved in intensive problem-solving. When the smoke cleared and things settled down, I remarked to her that her team seemed to have performed well in successfully bringing things back into control, but that it must have been a tremendously complicated event to have required so much fire power.

Her response was eye-opening. No, it wasn't a complicated event. To the contrary, this kind of thing happened frequently, and events just like this were taking up an increasingly large amount of their time. But most frustratingly of all, the entire event should have been handled by lower level employees who had the capacity and training to do so.

By this time, it was easy to see why this leadership team was less than successful. Instead of functioning at the strategic level the organization needed from them, they were spending a tremendous amount of time and high-level man and woman power putting out fires.

So why another book about leadership?
And why now?

Situations like the one above happen in companies every day. High-level leaders putting out fires that should be handled by other members of the team. Staff level workers wanting to grow, but not engaged in the solutions. Everyone busy, but not working up to their highest level of effectiveness.

Our belief at Associates For Professional Development (AFPD), our coaching and consulting firm, is that new, creative approaches to leadership are essential. Most of us are working harder, longer, and faster than ever before. Doing more with less. Taking on more responsibility as we streamline our companies and reduce the size of the workforce. We seem to live each day immersed in the important (and sometimes unimportant) tasks that come to define us. And still we carry with us that familiar feeling: "What did I really do today?"

The simple truth is that the need for healthy, effective leaders is growing, not waning. The faster we move, the more we look to the people around us for help, wisdom, mentoring, guidance. We look to our leaders to inspire us, to lead us to a place that makes all of the stress and hard work worth it. We want our leaders to give the work experience some meaning.

This is the answer to the question: "Why now?" and it is what led us to develop **The Leadership Nexus**. We wanted to find a way to help executives re-align themselves and their teams, to help them function at the highest levels of their expertise — to make sure that work is getting done at the right level, by the right people, at the right time.

Over the past 20 years there have been hundreds of books written on leadership and leadership development. Understanding the nature of leadership and recognizing what makes a good leader are vital to the ongoing development of organizations and the people within them.

Looking through a list of the writers of these books makes for an interesting trip down writer's lane — they come from all parts of the professional spectrum, successful business men and women, famous athletes and their coaches, academicians, consultants and coaches.

There is no lack of information on the topic of leadership. But what distinguishes one book from another, one approach or model from another? Certainly, the quality of the writing and the experience of the author are distinguishing factors. So is the approach the author takes.

But the distinguishing element is that most leadership books focus on one of two major themes:

- **Leader characteristics and qualities** — the skill-building component of leadership.
  Characteristics and behaviors are crucial to the implementation of successful leadership. Continual learning, positive energy, balance, and an ability to focus on strategy are essential to the success of any leader. So are identifying a shared vision, setting priorities, behaving with integrity, and being able to positively influence others. A charismatic leader has a degree of charm, enthusiasm or presence to which followers gravitate.

- **The approach taken** — the relationship component of leadership.
  Collaborative leaders are able to work with a wide variety of people to find solutions. Autocratic leaders are efficient and get things done regardless of the costs. Consensus builders create coalitions and bring teams together. But the approach leaders take also helps them define the types of relationships they have with their team members, their co-workers, their customers.

There is no question that these qualities and approaches are essential to leadership. But what we hear from our clients is that these alone do not touch on some of their critical leadership needs. For example, they express frustration at how quickly and frequently they get pulled into the weeds. They know that a strategic perspective is critical to their success, but they don't have the time to develop it. They often describe how frustrated they are at their inability to work to their highest abilities.

A glance at the leadership pyramid below provides a visual example of how these areas of focus relate to each other. At the top are the skills that leaders acquire as they grow. These skills are often the culmination of years of hard work in the leadership arena, and they can serve to separate the truly successful leaders from the not-so-successful.

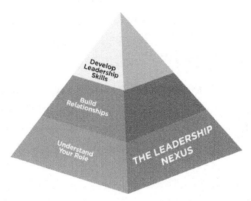

More fundamental and below these on the pyramid lies the ability to build helpful, effective relationships with external customers and clients, and more importantly, internally with team members, peers, and superiors. Without these relationships, getting things done is infinitely more difficult.

At the base, the foundation of the pyramid, however, lies the most basic of all the leadership elements: a deep understanding of and an appreciation for what their role will demand of them — an ability to appropriately engage their thoughts and their actions in ways that enable them to meet the leadership needs of their team.

This is the focus of **The Leadership Nexus**.

This gap between quality and approach, the development of a variety of leadership skills and the ability to work at the level that is most effective, is our major focus.

The Leadership Nexus takes a different slant on leadership development; one that is based upon a recognition that, for most people, some combination of thought and action is a necessity for success. However, and this is where it gets interesting, the thoughts and actions necessary for success at one level of an organization are functionally different from those at other levels.

All companies have a structure. That structure is generally defined by the levels necessary to get all of the organization's work done — everything from the creation of organizational strategy and direction down through the making of products or providing services. It is these levels, and the thoughts and actions they require, that form the core of **The Leadership Nexus**.

Each organizational level has leadership responsibilities. What is the nature of the work performed by the company president? What is the nature of the work of his or her chief lieutenants? What are the job responsibilities of the managers and the front-line personnel?

Above all, how are these responsibilities different? What determines a leader's success at any of these levels? Should they all be thinking about the same things, or should they actually be focused on different things?

Looking at the thoughts and actions of leaders at these levels, and where these thoughts and actions intersect (the nexus points), gives us a unique way of understanding why leaders at each level within an institution MUST function differently if they are to succeed.

The Leadership Nexus is based upon four basic principles:

1. **Effective leaders use their minds differently as they grow in experience and insight.** They develop a more sophisticated ability to use logic and reason as well as their emotions to

consider possible reactions to difficult situations. They use their accumulated wisdom to make decisions that will help them, their team members, and their organizations create successful solutions for complex problems.

2. **Effective leaders learn how to act in a way that is aligned with their thoughts and decisions.** They formulate visions of where they want to go and then they expend the proper amount of energy to get there.

3. Effective leaders think and act in ways that are aligned with the needs of the roles for which they are hired. Since each organizational level is different, the leadership needs must be different as well.

4. **Effective leaders recognize leadership opportunities when they appear.** We call these opportunities Leadership Moments. An outstanding leader knows how to spot them and how to act on them effectively.

In short, outstanding leaders make decisions with an effective internal thought process that uses their own, unique, combination of logic and emotion. They align these actions with their decisions in ways that are reflective of the needs of the level for which they are responsible. And they are always on the lookout for opportunities to continue their growth.

CHAPTER 2

The Leadership Nexus Approach

"Leadership and learning are indispensable to each other."

John F. Kennedy (1917 - 1963), speech prepared for delivery in
Dallas the day of his assassination, November 22, 1963

The Leadership Nexus is a unique way of looking at how two essential elements of leadership, thought and action, align.

Thought Time is the terminology used to describe the thinking that goes into the things that are most important to successful decision-making. Too much Thought Time on the wrong things makes effective decision-making extremely difficult.

Action Time is the companion element that focuses on actions that need to be taken. Actions that are focused on the most effective use of time, energy, and position are crucial to success. Action Time measures what the leader spends time doing throughout the work day. Working on the right things is productive and leads us to feel, at the end of the day, that our time has been used well. Working on things that direct reports should be doing or on things that are no longer our true responsibility can lead us to wonder what we have actually accomplished.

The overall objective of **The Leadership Nexus** is to provide leaders with the opportunity to learn more about both their thoughts and their actions, and to see how effectively these thoughts and actions align with each other.

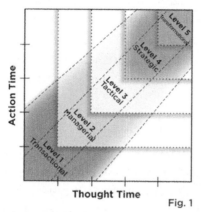

Fig. 1

Thought Time and Action Time alignment is represented by the five levels found on the chart (Fig. 1). The five levels are: *Transactional, Managerial, Tactical, Strategic, and Transformational.* Each level is important and has its own roles, characteristics, functions and risks.

Each of the five Leadership Nexus Levels is vital to the overall success of an organization, because each level has a set of essential functions. When these functions are performed well, success is possible because it has the capacity to meet its mission while also maintaining an ability to look into the future. It can remain sustainable, viable, and competitive.

However, each level of leadership is fundamentally different. Each has a distinct role to play, and each one requires a different set of skills in order for the work of that level to be done effectively.

Level 1: Transactional Leader

Level 1 **Transactional** leadership is where the most basic work gets done. Workers at this level perform concrete, routine, daily assigned tasks, generally the most hands-on work in the organization. They frequently manage day-to-day activities and deal with emergencies as they arise. The leadership is often supervisory and sometimes informal. But Transactional leaders step up as the need arises, lead through a particular situation, and then return to the work at hand.

Examples of Transactional leaders are easy to see. They are the individuals who work on the front lines of any organization. They do their jobs every day; looking for new problems to solve to make their corner of the workplace a little bit better for themselves and their co-workers. They often lead on the front lines without recognizing how important they are.

Characteristics
- A strong focus on the daily demands of the job.
- Work hard to do the best job possible, but often unable to catch up.
- Reacting to what happens in the surrounding environment.
- Seeing new processes as threats to tradition and/or stability.
- Generally low risk-taking with a preference to remain with procedures that have been successful in the past.

Level 2: Managerial Leader

Level 2 **Managerial** leaders are often in a first official leadership position. Their primary role is to balance daily work tasks with the management of staff. As a result, they often describe themselves as stretched between their own work responsibilities and the personal and professional demands of the team.

Successful Level 2 leaders promote worker efficiency, high stability and low chaos. They manage the inevitable conflicts that arise in busy workplaces. They may not like the conflict, but neither do they hide from it. **Managerial** leaders generally focus on short term immediate responsibilities.

As the need for change within an organization grows, the fundamental challenges to daily work shift. Consequently, **Managerial** leaders often find themselves under increasing pressure to move faster and to do more with their teams; often with the same or fewer resources.

Characteristics

- Maintain a balance between task and staff issues.
- Motivate staff to get work done efficiently and effectively.
- Develop positive relationships with staff without blurring relationship boundaries.
- Hold staff accountable.
- Resolve conflicts with minimal side effects.

Level 3: Tactical Leader

Level 3 **Tactical** leaders are responsible for larger groups of staff and the procedures that define their work. They operate at the intersection of strategy and tactics. **Tactical** leaders understand the complexities of daily work and excel at evaluating process effectiveness. They often spend their time resolving systemic issues and implementing new unit or departmental initiatives. They know where energies need to be focused. Often associated with middle management, they function at the departmental level where both strategy and operations are daily realities.

How do you identify an effective Level 3 **Tactical** leader? In large organizations, they will often make up the core group of mid-level management. These individuals are good at listening to what their bosses need and at understanding the strategic directions that are handed down to them. They may have a hand in developing some of that strategic vision or in articulating to the higher-ups how that vision may impact staff.

Successful **Tactical** leaders are equally good at communicating vision to their own teams. They inspire their managers and other team members to accomplish things they didn't know they were capable of doing. Even if they disagree with a strategic direction, they know how to get behind a decision and implement it with a minimum of disruption and a maximum of buy-in from staff.

Characteristics
- Comfortable with both operations and strategy.
- Manage short-term and long-term operations.
- Flexible and adaptable as they adjust to constant changes.
- Get out quickly when pulled into the weeds
- Hold individuals and teams accountable.

Level 4: Strategic Leader

Level 4 **Strategic** leaders create a vision for the organization along with an understanding of what the various teams will need to do in order to reach it. Level 4 leaders need a high tolerance for risk and change and they spend quite a bit of time talking, meeting, and kicking things around before actually putting strategies into action.

Successful **Strategic** leaders have a comfort with and an ability to look into the future. Above all, they can articulate an over-arching strategy and are able to inspire the confidence and enthusiasm necessary for the strategy to succeed. Although many leaders at this level do not begin with these abilities, they find that developing them is essential.

Characteristics

- Spend most of their time in strategic development.
- Think long-term and rarely get into the weeds.
- Build structures that enable them to easily and effectively delegate tasks.
- Develop strong relationships to facilitate creative problem-solving.
- Comfortable with conflict and use it positively.
- Adaptable, creative thinkers and systemic actors.

Level 5: Transformational Leader

Level 5 **Transformational** leaders spend a great deal of time picturing how to change the very nature of an organization. They immerse themselves in their vision and work with those who are in the vanguard of these changes.

Transformational leaders are highly energized, rarely take no for an answer and are always looking for a better, more elegant solution. Level 5 leaders develop relationships across intellectual and organizational boundaries. They feed themselves with new insights, inventions, and initiatives.

Cross-industry relationships stimulate the growth of a Transformational leader and serve as early-warning systems for their initiatives. Being a **Transformational** leader also means being comfortable with risk-taking. Spectacular failures can sometimes be the result, but the drive to move toward a new future is more powerful than the risk of failure.

The greatest vulnerability of a **Transformational** leader is a failure of creativity. Failure of initiatives is fine; just change directions. Failure of processes is okay; create new ones. But a failure of creativity can lead to catastrophe.

Characteristics

- Relentless change agents hungry for information.
- See a future that few others can see
- Desire to radically change their part of the world.
- Recognize how new developments outside of the industry can impact where the industry could go.
- Do not mind failure because failure is just another step toward success.
- Enjoy breaking things that are not broken and putting them back together in new, unique ways.

How to Use The Leadership Nexus

There are two primary ways to use The Leadership Nexus Assessment. First, it can be used to clarify the leadership demands at each level of an organization and to identify the corresponding skills necessary for leader success. The activities provided in this book will help strengthen existing leadership skills and assist in developing new ones.

Second, The Leadership Nexus Assessment can be used to measure how much time and energy an individual is currently spending on each individual set of leadership levels. Regardless of position, a leader can use this score to better understand what constitutes higher level thinking and to challenge their growth by better understanding what it means to work at the top of their degree or license.

Like most assessments of this type, The Leadership Nexus is appropriately understood as a snapshot of an individual's leadership at the time it was taken, so the nexus point may or may not be different a month or a year from now. The assessment is best used to help grow leadership capacities today, and to help continue that growth tomorrow and beyond.

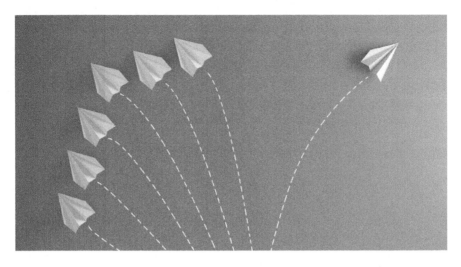

CHAPTER 3

How can I use The Leadership Nexus to become a better leader?

"The pessimist complains about the wind. The optimist expects it to change. The leader adjusts the sails."

John Maxwell

The point of **The Leadership Nexus** is to have a useful model of leadership that anyone can use to grow their leadership capacities. So, let's dive into three practical areas that can impact leadership immediately: Roles, Questions, and Risk.

Roles

Every level of leadership performs a different role. Think for a moment about the US Army, one of the strongest, most ably-led organizations in the world. Where does leadership show up here?

When I did my stint in the Army back in the 70s, the first thing I learned was that my drill sergeant was my leader. He was in charge of every daily function that occurred during those first eight weeks, and it quickly became clear that my very life could depend on my ability to follow his instructions.

He led with an iron fist, but also with an understanding of how to get the most out of each recruit. That was his job — the role that he was tasked to play. And he did it well!

Eventually, our sergeant identified squad leaders, internal leaders who helped encourage and lead our fellow recruits. Mostly these were either natural leaders, or they were the stronger, more capable members of the squad that the others looked up to.

Although it felt like my drill sergeant was the ultimate boss, it was clear that he was not. He had a captain, the company commander, who oversaw a set of platoons. The captain's role was to make certain that all his sergeants trained us well, and that we performed our jobs efficiently, effectively, and with enthusiasm! He supervised our training, and he made sure that all of the drill sergeants were teaching the same skills in the same way and getting the same results.

Above the captain was a major and above him a colonel. Although at the time I had no idea what they did, I eventually came to learn that they determined all of the training procedures, changing things as the needs of the army shifted. Their role was to ensure that all of the soldiers and recruits at the base were performing up to the expectations of the general who was in charge of the entire base.

So what was the point of each of these leaders? Each had a job to do, a role to play within the context of the base and within the context of the US Army. Each one performed his role well. Each of them contributed in their individual ways to the development of a raw recruit into an effective soldier.

A recruit. A squad leader. A sergeant. A captain. A colonel. A general. Each leadership level performing a vital function, each of them distinctly different from the others. This is a great example of how leadership actually functions in an organization. The names are different. The titles vary. But the roles of each level are still crucial.

Each of the five levels in **The Leadership Nexus** has a unique role. Let's look at them.

Level 1: Transactional Leader

The role of a **Transactional** leader is to lead within the team. This is the very definition of being in the weeds, because these are the weeds. Leaders at this level can be formal or titled, such as supervisor or team lead. They can also be informal; for example, a strong performer who is looked up to by other members of the staff.

Transactional leaders are important because they are closest to the work. In emergencies they are the individuals who are most often followed. They are the consummate firefighters, leading fellow firefighters, taking care of the team and putting out the fire. Look for a moment at what happens in an emergency. A machine breaks, a patient falls, a crisis arises. Who is the first to respond? Who takes charge of the situation and manages it until it is either handled or until someone with situational expertise arrives? This is the **Transactional** leader.

Whether they are formal or informal, titled or self-identified, people follow them. Even if they don't see themselves as leaders, they are.

Level 2: Managerial Leader

A Level 2 **Managerial** leader is often in a first formal leadership position. Like the army sergeant, they are responsible for their team, and their role is to ensure that daily tasks are completed effectively with a minimum of conflict and concern.

Managerial Leaders may be in the weeds with their team, but they are the ones responsible for making sure that team members are properly trained, up to the task, and doing their jobs. They are responsible for holding their people accountable, and they are expected to handle conflicts that arise within the team.

It is this tension between task completion and staff member interactions that often creates the most role difficulty for **Managerial** Leaders. Taking care of tasks is generally more satisfying (and often more fun) than managing conflict; but not taking care of conflict eventually creates longer-term problems.

Level 3: Tactical Leader

Since Level 3 **Tactical** leaders work at the intersection of strategy and tactics, they are tasked with having the skill to understand and lead from the bigger picture. Whether natural or developed, this strategic focus is the key to success for the **Tactical** leader.

Adaptability, vision, and insight are all essential skills for level 3 leaders. So is the ability to inspire large groups and to operationalize complex processes. The **Tactical** leader's role is to make sure that all team members have the resources and skills necessary to effectively carry out the strategic initiatives of the organization.

While a **Tactical** leader may be pulled into the weeds in an emergency, it is essential that they recognize when this is happening and have the ability to pull back as quickly as possible.

They must maintain their grasp of the bigger picture. This leader is working in both the present and the future, balancing the very different demands of each.

Level 4: Strategic Leader

Level 4 **Strategic** leaders live primarily in the future. Their role in the organization is to create direction: a clear picture of where it is going and how it will get there. The most effective **Strategic** leaders have an understanding, a vision, of the industry, how it is changing over time and what the staff will need in order to compete in this future.

Strategic leaders need time and space to create, commodities that seem to be in increasingly short supply. Setting clear boundaries around their use of time is essential. With those boundaries, they can create high-performance teams that are able to weather all storms and manage the daily crises that come at them. Without these boundaries, **Strategic** leaders often describe themselves as deep in the weeds, ineffective, or frustrated.

Good **Strategic** leaders walk a fine line between being appreciated and respected by their teams and being recognized as hard drivers who can make sense out of uncertain futures.

Level 5: Transformational Leader

Level 5 **Transformational** leaders break things that aren't broken. They change things that are stable. They create new things out of the ashes of the old or sometimes out of seemingly thin air. The force of their vision, and often their personality, can be difficult to resist.

The role of **Transformational** leaders is to shake things up. When done well, there is an understanding of trends and technological advances that is not always apparent to everyone else. Blending these trends and advances into a coherent vision of the future of both the company and the industry is what drives them. And even if we don't always understand where they are going, they will take us there anyway.

Transformational leaders embrace change and the upheaval that comes from it. They develop a strength of will that spills over to everyone around them. They believe in themselves and the people who work with them. They build stability out of chaos; often the chaos they themselves create. They are responsible for the macro changes that re-define entire industries, even cultures. Often admired and sometimes reviled, their role is to point us in new directions and inspire us to go there with them.

Summing Up

When you get right down to it, in order to be truly effective, a leader needs to appropriately align the skills and talents they possess with the needs of the role into which they have been hired. As the role changes, the leadership requirements will need to change as well. Align them well and success often follows. Align them poorly and buckle up for a bumpy ride.

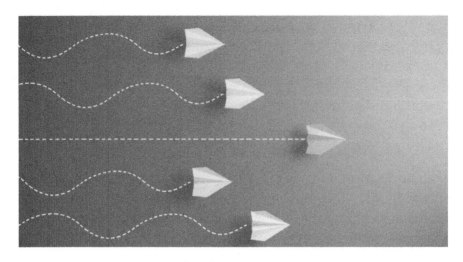

CHAPTER 4

Leadership Questions

"When you're a contributor you try to have all the answers. When you're a leader, your job is to have all the questions."

Jack Welch

We believe that effective leaders are not defined by the instructions they give or by the problems they solve. They are defined by the nature of the questions they ask.

Let's repeat that: The most effective leaders are the ones who know the right questions to ask, of the right people, at the right times.

Why does this make them more effective? Because it helps them challenge the thinking of everyone around them. It helps them help others grow. It brings others' talents to the forefront where those talents can be leveraged to solve problems. It utilizes the best of everyone around them and encourages everyone to be engaged in solving problems, not just following orders.

Since each level has a different focus, it is reasonable to expect that the questions asked at each level will differ as well. One of the basic elements of **The Leadership Nexus** is that it helps leaders identify these essential questions.

Level 1: Transactional Leader Questions

At the **Transactional** level, Level 1, the most important questions asked are also the most fundamental. They tend to focus on the basic elements of who, what, when, where, and why. What is broken? Who broke it? What do we do next?

These are the questions that enable basic problems to be solved. Without them, essential work doesn't get done. Things don't move. **Transactional** leaders are constantly asking these basic questions because this is what resolves their most pressing problems.

Effective **Transactional** leaders want the people around them to be active participants in the work so that things get done when they need to be done while making sure they have each other's backs.

As a result, **Transactional** leader questions will often be designed to bond them with their co-workers:

- What do we need to do?
- Is this a problem we have seen before?
- What did we do with it then?
- Will you help me with this?
- What did our training teach us about this situation?
- Who was responsible for this?
- Where are the tools we need to fix this?

Whether they are functioning as formal or informal leaders, **Transactional** Leaders are interested in the basics. This is what makes them so important on the front lines.

Level 2: Managerial Leader Questions

When Transactional leaders move up to the **Managerial** level, their role changes. Since responsibility at this level is now divided between focus on the well-being of the team as well as on getting work done, it also means that the questions they ask must be different.

Level 2 **Managerial** leaders find themselves asking questions about the growth and health of the team. "What can I do to help you with this problem?" is a perfect example. This question sets the expectation that the team member will be solving the problem, not the manager. It also says the leader is there to help the team member use his/her own physical and intellectual resources to take care of the situation.

"What resources do you need?" and "What do you need from me to help you?" are other examples of **Managerial** leader questions. Since the manager is often not the person who will (or should) be handling the problem, ensuring that the team members have the resources they need demonstrates both trust in the team member's ability to do the job and that the team member can trust the leader to provide the necessary resources while staying out of the way while they do it.

This is what engagement really looks like: both leader and team member actively engaged in solving a problem, each using their unique resources and abilities and trusting each other to play their individual parts.

Level 2 Managerial leaders are also responsible for looking ahead and preparing their team members for future problems.

So another set of questions focuses on prevention and preparation.

- How can we prevent this next time?
- What can I do to help you with this situation?
- Are we staffed appropriately?
- Do we have the necessary budgetary support?
- What is the basic strategic direction I am hearing from my one-up that I need to pass on to my team?
- How do we blend these new initiatives into our current processes?
- How do I make sure that my team is ready for this? Budget, strategic direction, staffing, communication.

Budget, strategic direction, staffing, communication. These are all elements of **Managerial** leadership. Shifting their thoughts and actions from their own success to the well-being and success of the team is what defines an effective Level 2 leader.

Level 3: Tactical Leader Questions

Because Level 3 **Tactical** leaders work at the intersection of strategy and tactics, their vision is constantly moving between communications from above (the strategic direction of the organization) and below (how staff is handling these strategic initiatives, projects, and directions).

A **Tactical** leader asks larger, more probing questions than leaders at the previous two levels. "Why did this problem happen in the first place?" "What were the root causes of this situation?" "What can we change to avoid a recurrence of this problem?" These types of questions are best asked after a problem has been solved, since they are oriented toward the future rather than the immediate past.

Effective Level 3 **Tactical** leaders recognize that the timing of their questions is important. Ask expansive questions too early and energy is prematurely shifted away from problem-solving. This can be confusing to staff members, causing them uncertainty around their own priorities and how to meet them. Ask them too late and the incentive to change disappears — out of sight, out of mind.

Successful **Tactical** leaders are focused on discovering how a process or policy can be changed in order to shift the team from short-term problem-solving to longer-term strategic change.

- How does this solution align with our overall strategic direction?
- What can we do to strengthen our efficiency?
- Is it possible for us to work in new ways that reduce or eliminate waste or ineffectiveness?
- The strategic direction of the company requires us to focus on revenue enhancement over the next six months. What do we need to change in our team processes that will help us achieve this goal?

These questions are designed to help staff maintain a focus on the larger issue of how current actions will lead to a desired future. When **Tactical** leaders get pulled into the weeds, they are generally diving back into the past and present, asking questions that are designed to solve a present-day problem rather than a future one.

By presenting this type of question to team leaders, the **Tactical** leader challenges the team to grow in problem-solving ability, creativity, insight, and forward thinking. Is this an easy shift? Absolutely not! But it is the kind of approach that challenges teams to grow.

Level 4: Strategic Leader Questions

Strategic leaders are ultimately responsible for the direction in which their organization, or their portion of it, moves. Thought time, meetings with other **Strategic** leaders, reading about and watching how markets move are all key tasks for Level 4 leaders. And their questions are designed to stimulate this type of thinking.

A **Strategic** leader asks large questions that focus on where the organization is headed over time. These questions help the organization make sense of the direction in which it is moving as well as how everyday tasks can be aligned to accomplish this.

- If we re-thought our approach, what could we do differently to change how we accomplish this task?
- How can we realign operations to more effectively achieve our strategic goals over the next several years?

Strategic leaders also recognize the importance of challenging relationships to reflect a focus on the future.

- How can we positively influence other leaders within the organization to respect our value?
- If we implemented this solution, who else would it affect and how would it affect them?
- What initiatives do we need to undertake this year to help us achieve our organizational goals?

These are the types of questions that ask, and sometimes demand, that team members shift their focus from the daily, reaction-oriented quest to get things done to the much harder questions: *"Why are we doing it this way and how can we break this down in order to create something new?"*

Level 5: Transformational Leader Questions

Transformational leaders are disruptors. By their very nature, **Transformational** leaders want to build larger, more interesting organizations. Their questions are designed to create a disruptive strategic direction, because they recognize that this disruption is what causes new things to happen.

- Is there another approach that would enable us to solve more than one problem at a time?
- Why are we doing this work in the same way it has been done for years?
- How can we use emerging technologies in our company and in our industry?

Level 5 questions challenge existing modes of thought. They attempt to move people into dramatically new ways of thinking and working. They also communicate the vibrancy and aliveness of the **Transformational** leader. Without this, the future can be a pretty frightening place. With it, all involved will have somewhere to go that is exciting and alive with possibilities.

- Who do we not know that we need to get to know?
- Are you able to see where my vision could take us and will you go there with me?

These are examples of questions that focus on the invisible. They are asking team members to see things that can be difficult, even frightening, to see. But this is what makes **Transformational** leaders transformational. They challenge all of us to see beyond ourselves into a new and different future.

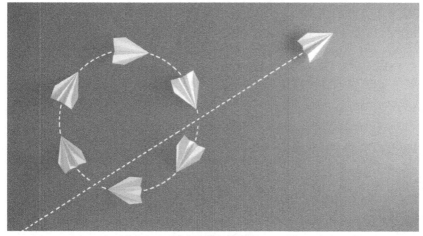

CHAPTER 5

Understanding Risk

"The secret to my success is that I bit off more than I could chew and chewed as fast as I could."

Paul Hogan

Risk is an interesting lens through which to look at leadership. What do we risk when we think about changing a policy or a process? What do we risk when we think about implementing a radically new idea? What do we risk when we ask a difficult question instead of solving a problem ourselves?

Just as the roles and questions of each level differ, so do the risks incurred by leaders as they move through the various levels. If we return to the military example for just a moment, let's ask this question: "What does a private risk when making a decision on the front line in the heat of battle, and how is that different from a decision made by a general in the same battle?"

A decision made by a private is likely to most directly affect his or her own life and the lives of the individuals around them — their fellow squad members. The risk is fairly contained to these individuals. This decision could directly affect the outcome of a particular part of a battle, but not often the outcome of an entire battle.

A general who makes a decision in the heat of the same battle risks the lives of all of the troops under their command. A single strategic decision can put at risk an entire platoon, company, or battalion. While the general's life is usually not at stake, he or she is risking the lives of a great many soldiers as well as the potential outcome of an entire war.

This is the nature of risk. The closer a leader is to the core function of an organization, the more personal the risk. The higher the level of leadership, the more systemic that risk becomes. A private risks his or her own life and the lives of his or her buddies. A general risks the lives of an entire battalion.

What is important to understand about this concept of risk is that **all risk is important, but the nature of the risk changes.** And why is this important? Because human beings are risk-calculating creatures. We are always measuring risk, even when we aren't aware that we are. Why do leaders make certain decisions? The answer can often be traced back to the type of risk they perceive themselves to be taking.

Level 1: Transactional Leader

Level 1 leadership is about accuracy and stability; creating and maintaining a stable, efficient workplace with understandable rules and reasonable policies and procedures. A Level 1 **Transactional** leader runs the greatest risk by making task mistakes and by failing to accomplish these tasks in a timely and efficient manner.

Transactional leaders often feel at risk when their visibility goes up, because this is precisely when task mistakes can most easily be seen. A leader who bubbles into visibility because of outstanding work can also be noticed when something goes wrong.

As coaches, we frequently run into this when talking with front line leaders who say something like, "I just want to keep my head down and do a good job. I don't want any fuss over what I do. I just do my work and I do it well. But heaven help me if I make a mistake — it's like the world came to an end!"

This is not only a statement of pride in doing a good job. It is also a recognition of the risk inherent when that good job isn't quite so good. Because the bottom line is that this is how they can lose their job.

Effective Level 1 **Transactional** leaders recognize this risk of visibility and are able to work with it and with their teammates to produce quality outcomes with a minimum of errors. This type of risk can be highly motivating to some individuals — for others it can be overwhelming.

Level 2: Managerial Leader

Level 2 leadership is about building effective teams. Many first-time **Managerial** leaders are promoted because of their technical abilities, so their struggles often lie in developing their teams and team members.

Managerial leaders who move up from within the team face a two-fold problem: how do I stop being a friend and become a boss; and, how do I learn how to build my team — a skill that is very different from being part of the team and just doing a good job.

This is why the Managerial leader's highest risk lies in the areas of team-building, accountability, development, and effective use of resources. All of these crucial to the development of a high-performing team. And without the development of the team, the work is at risk.

A great example of this is found in the manager who was promoted from within and had an existing group of friends on the team. Once in the new role, if the manager maintains those friendships as they were, talk of favoritism and unfairness often emerge and staff cooperation and teamwork can drop.

Adapting to a role that is different from that of team member and friend can make creating a clear set of boundaries and holding staff members accountable difficult. But without this adaptation, the manager cannot create a high-performing team. The risk is two-fold: risk not being seen as "one of us"; risk not holding team members accountable and developing the team.

Level 3: Tactical Leader

Level 3 leadership is about balance. Since Level 3 **Tactical** leaders are generally responsible for larger sets of teams, they are most vulnerable to a lack of adaptability, creativity or confidence. Knowing how to balance competing needs, competing budgets, competing agendas; these are the things that keep them up at night.

Balancing the strategic needs of the organization with the specific needs of various teams is a difficult challenge. And this is where the **Tactical** leader's risk lies. Balance these competing needs well and multiple departments run smoothly. Struggle with this, and a great number of people are unhappy.

Picture a director whose one-up is pushing for programmatic change in an attempt to bring the organization into a more competitive stance in the market, but whose direct reports are complaining about a lack of clarity and direction, smaller budgets and less staff. What a balancing act!

Risk at this level tends to be less personal and more systemic or programmatic. Most **Tactical** leaders will not lose their jobs if a single initiative fails. Neither will the front line workers. But the company or its reputation can be at risk with the failure of this same initiative. And, over time, the **Tactical** leader's reputation (and job) will be at risk if there are too many failures.

A leader who can maintain this balance while keeping the boss satisfied and direct reports engaged is a truly valuable commodity. Recognizing that this is the area of greatest risk enables the Level 3 leader to build the skills necessary to pull this off.

Level 4: Strategic Leader

Level 4 leadership is about strategy. A Level 4 **Strategic** leader is deeply committed to the long-term development of the organization; so, the ability to accurately see into the future is vital. This is the **Strategic** leader's greatest risk — a lack of vision.

If the leader's vision is correct, the result is growth, viability, and financial stability. If this vision is wrong, the result can be organizational failure. Given the scale of decision-making at this level, a **Strategic** Leader must have the courage to act, often with less than full information.

When Dwight D. Eisenhower planned for the D-Day invasion during WWII, he could see all of the pieces on the chessboard — not only his own, but also those of Germany. His understanding of how and when all of those pieces needed to move, and how to keep all of the coalition leaders invested led him, and the Allies, to a tremendous victory; one that changed the direction of the war.

The personal risk that General Eisenhower faced was very different from the risk of one of the troops landing on the beaches of Normandy. His life was not at risk, but his reputation as a commanding general most certainly was, as were the lives of all of his troops.

This type of risk occurs every day in business. Level 4 leaders read the tea leaves of the future and make decisions that risk everything. This is what they do.

Level 5: Transformational Leader

Level 5 leadership is about game changing. **Transformational** leaders embrace change and the upheaval that comes from it. They develop a strength of will that spills over to everyone who comes into contact with them. And they believe in themselves and the people who work with them.

The risks associated with sailing in uncharted waters, in trying new technologies, in creating new industries or a new organization are very high. It takes an individual with a strong sense of self as well as a fundamental belief in the correctness of the vision to pull this off successfully.

The ambiguity inherent and associated risks in these new approaches is often enough to keep talented visionaries from moving to this game-changing position; but when it is managed well, it is a sight to behold.

When Christopher Columbus set out for the new world, he trusted a level of vision that was well beyond that of other travelers of the day. He not only transformed an understanding of how to reach other parts of the world, he also demonstrated the power of setting forth into the unknown. He completed this while facing incredible risks and it led to amazing rewards.

Steve Jobs accomplished the same feat in his uncompromising approach to technological innovation. In his drive toward excellence, he transformed not only computers, but also the music industry, the telephone industry, and the movie business.

But we don't have to be a Steve Jobs or a Christopher Columbus to be a Level 5 leader within our own organizations. **Transformational** leaders develop an ability to look beyond their own limits and the limits of everyone around them. They are able to see how big pieces fit together, how changing one part of a system can lead to inevitable changes in the rest of it.

What is at risk at this level is: everything. All of the project financing. The jobs of all the people who have signed on to the vision. The reputation for being a **Transformational** leader. All of these things are at risk. But for the **Transformational** leader, it is precisely this risk, this shoving of all the chips into the pot, that creates the excitement that fuels the passion for transformation.

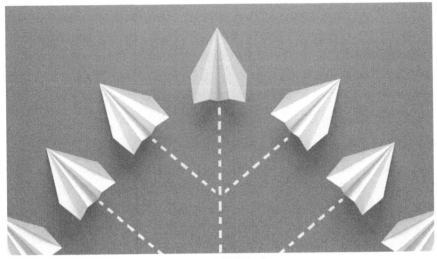

CHAPTER 6

Functioning at the Top of Your Level

> *"Management is doing things right; leadership*
> *is doing the right things."*
>
> Peter Drucker

How can I operate at the top of my license? We hear this question quite often from our coaching clients. And, as we have seen, operating at the top of their game is actually a matter of clearly understanding the role they have been hired to play and knowing which questions are most appropriate to ask.

The purpose of **The Leadership Nexus** is to help individual leaders more effectively align their thoughts and actions, especially as they relate to the roles they have been selected to perform. So begin by reflecting on what you are being paid to do — really being paid to do; not just what you feel most comfortable doing.

This kind of honest reflection requires plenty of hard work:

- Asking better questions.

- Spending extra time evaluating what your role actually needs from you.

- Recognizing when you are diving into the weeds, how long to remain there, and when to elevate back out of them.

- Remembering that the higher the level, the more you must rely on others to get work done.

- Respecting the types of risks that are inherent at your level and being willing to act on them.

As you strengthen your alignment of the thoughts and actions necessary for your leadership level, it becomes easier to remain there when appropriate and to move to another level when required.

Most of us approach a leadership role by focusing on what we need to do to be successful. "Oh, if I do this, my team will appreciate it. If I do that, my boss will notice how well I am doing."

But what if we were to reverse this thought process and start instead with: what does my position need most from me?

This is a totally different proposition, because it moves from the outside in — from the leadership qualities most needed for success at a given position.

Think of it like this. What are the most important deliverables for a military general? How do they differ from the deliverables for a successful sergeant? How is it that these two are so completely different?

This is not just about what the team needs. It is also about what the position needs from its leader for the team members to be successful and for work to be completed effectively and efficiently.

Let's take a look at each of the levels to see what this looks like from the perspective of both the team members' needs and the position needs.

Level 1: Transactional Leadership Level

Team members at this level are close to their team leaders, because the leaders are often an integral part of the team. Generally speaking, this level requires its leaders to be able to function both as a part of the team and also outside the team. Not always an easy balancing act.

What do the team members need? They need their leader to be an essential part of the team, serving as a spokesperson, answering front-line questions about work and personnel, adding support and solving problems.

But what does the position require of the leader? The position needs the team leader to help other team members solve problems they can't solve on their own. It needs them to help team members stay on track and to produce the work product (whatever that might be) with as much ease and efficiency as possible. In short, the position needs the leader to help the team members get where they need to be in terms of production.

Often these leaders are serving in an unofficial capacity. They may not have been promoted to this position of responsibility, but they have been elevated to it based upon the strength of their performance, their personality, or both. Due to this increased visibility, informal leaders in this position may find themselves identified as high performers and possible candidates for promotion — even if that is not what they are most interested in.

Level 2: Managerial Leadership Level

Successful teams are often led by an individual who is both a great worker and an effective formal leader. This leader either knows how or learns how to balance excellent work with an ability to manage the intricacies of conflict, accountability, leadership, and communication.

What the team members need from a Managerial leader is an individual who is good at clarifying work rules and responsibilities, removing operational barriers, and keeping track of the budget. They need the Managerial leader to push them forward to their higher-ups and to defend them at the same time. They need them to answer their questions, but to also stay one step ahead of any potential changes so that those changes don't disrupt the daily routine any more than absolutely necessary.

What the position requires from the Managerial leader is all of the above, but also accountability, inspiration, and consistency. Good Managerial leaders excel at removing or reducing barriers. They effectively manage conflict, and they are always on the lookout for ways to grow both the individual team members and the team as a whole.

The balance between inspiring the team and holding them accountable for both their production and their work with other team members is often a very difficult thing. When Managerial leaders are promoted from within, they then have the complicated task of re-establishing themselves as bosses with individuals who previously related to them in an entirely different way.

If this re-definition of roles does not occur, the leader invariably winds up in a real pickle: unable to hold team members accountable and splitting the loyalties of the various team members. Understanding how to manage the conflict that naturally arises when people work closely together is critical to this leader's success. Otherwise, the conflicts continue to fester and often get worse.

When the re-definition does occur, however, both the leader and the team members can flourish. Conflict is addressed quickly and effectively, growth can take place, and everyone understands who is what to whom.

Level 3: Tactical Leadership Level

Departments function best when leaders trust their staff to do their jobs and allow them the space to do them well. Staff members can then trust their leaders to provide them with the appropriate strategic direction, the budgets to execute, and the structure that best enables them to move in that direction.

Teams and team members need their Tactical leaders to be clear about strategy, but also to know how to represent them up the chain of command. They need their leaders to be able to jump into the weeds when absolutely necessary, but respect them enough to jump right back out, providing time and space to solve problems on their own.

The position, however, requires more than this. Outstanding Tactical leaders not only manage problems and people well, they also inspire their team members to grow and to excel at their jobs. They build strong leaders who are capable of implementing the strategies of the senior executives. They hold their teams accountable for their production or for their service delivery.

Above all, the successful Tactical leader must build a culture of growth, development, initiative, and accountability. This is what inspires team members to deliver results that consistently surpass expectations.

Level 4: Strategic Leadership Level

Successful companies consistently balance themselves between working toward a future that encourages growth and expansion and a present that is grounded in the realities of budget, personnel, production, and process. Leaders at the strategic level understand that this balance requires them to be equally adept at looking into the future while always keeping an eye on the present. **Personnel who report to a Strategic leader need that leader to be able to create a vision of the future** that is both challenging and attainable. They want to know that their leader knows where they are going and can inspire them to go there together.

What the position requires is someone who can think creatively while communicating across multiple roles and positions. Additionally, they must manage a wide variety of personalities and agendas, and keep their leaders focused on what must be achieved.

Strategic leaders often find themselves in a position where they must convince others that a particular direction is, indeed, the best way to proceed. They must understand how to encourage support, build consensus, generate enthusiasm, and manage a wide variety of personalities and multiple agendas.

Successful Strategic leaders benefit greatly from a well-developed ability to understand people and how to get them to buy into a particular vision. This people-ability is often the "secret sauce," the thing that makes it all work.

Level 5: Transformational Leadership Level

Transformational leaders are in the business of creating the companies of the future. Their workers need them to create a roadmap that can be used to move the organization through this change and they need an inspirational and/or aspirational message that they can hold on to. These messages are the glue that keeps the Transformational leader connected to the rest of the team.

What the position needs from a Transformation leader is considerably different. Success at this level requires the leader to have a deep understanding of the shifting tides of the marketplace, to see where the organization fits into that marketplace, and to lay out how the organization will get there.

This requires a broad vision that encompasses multiple disciplines and an ability to see beyond the current horizon. It demands a well-crafted ability to understand how advances in one area can affect advances in another. And it requires an element of risk-taking that can be daunting to the faint-of-heart, because the stakes are so high. It is the embodiment of high risk, high reward.

Leading at this level requires a well-developed sense of creativity along with a strong reading of risk versus reward. With a healthy balance, a Transformational leader can take an organization to amazing heights. Without it, they crash and burn.

Not all organizations need their top leaders to be transformational. And not all Transformational leaders succeed in their quests. But when it works, it is something to behold.

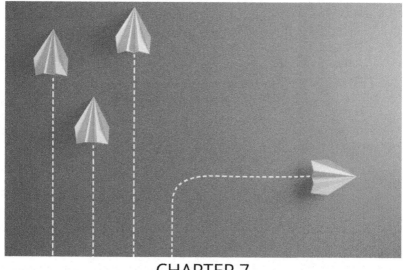

CHAPTER 7

Leadership Moments

> *"Character may be manifested in the great moments, but it is made in the small ones."*
>
> Winston Churchill

Leadership is not a quality, nor is it an event. It is the ability to recognize those moments when we have the opportunity to act in a way that positively affects the needs of the people and situations around us.

Each day we are presented with multiple opportunities for this kind of action. Many of them small, a few are larger, and a small number are truly critical. Recognizing these opportunities and acting on them in appropriate, helpful ways is what makes a leader great.

These are what we call **Leadership Moments**. Leadership Moments are decision points, moments in the course of a day when you have the opportunity to decide to lead or not. They are times when you can choose to dive back into what has always worked for you, or struggle to try something different. These Leadership Moments have three characteristics. They:

1. most effectively help resolve an immediate situation,

2. assist the team members in their personal and professional growth; and,

3. advance the needs of the team and the organization.

Each of these three characteristics is important in its own way. But when they work together, they provide a powerful expression of positive leadership.

The first of these is an **effective resolution of an immediate situation**. For example, a team member comes to her supervisor, again, with a complaint that her co-worker is spending company time talking on the phone about an ongoing family problem. As a result, she is unable to get her work completed and it then falls to this individual to get it done so that she can carry on with her own work.

What is the decision point for the supervisor? Does she half-listen to her team member because she has heard this complaint several times before and, after talking to the individual involved, was assured that it wouldn't happen again? Or does she engage her active listening skills and realize that she needs to take a different kind of action in order to manage this more effectively so that it actually stops?

It is so much easier to just make the situation go away. But is this the most effective solution? Probably not. Instead, perhaps it is time for the supervisor to have an engaged conversation with the offending team member about how her family situation is creating problems for other members of her team, and that the two of them need to identify some creative solutions so that she can go back to being an effective team member.

This is the kind of decision that can be easily ignored, at least for a period of time. But it almost always grows into a larger problem that will take considerably more time, energy, and focus to solve the larger it gets. Finding a final resolution to the current situation ensures that it will not happen anymore. The team members both get what they need, and the supervisor is finally able to put to rest an ongoing problem that is undercutting the team's performance.

The second element of a Leadership Moment is that it **assists the team members in their personal and professional growth**. In the previous example the supervisor has the opportunity to attempt a resolution that respects the team member's problems at home and simultaneously helps her grow in her ability to set appropriate boundaries around work and home and to find creative solutions that will actually help resolve them.

The leadership opportunity for this supervisor lies in her ability to use this family problem as a vehicle to help her team member grow and to learn how to more effectively balance her personal and professional lives.

The third characteristic of a Leadership Moment is that it **advances the needs of the team and the organization**. Finding a more robust solution to the problem above contributes to the development of the team member while also getting back some of the work time that has been lost to the ongoing crisis.

As a result, everybody wins: the team member finally discovers a way to resolve the larger family problem, the team gets back some of its work time and focus, and the company is no longer paying an employee for time not spent on company business. Additionally, the team has now grown stronger and the leader has enhanced the respect for her that she needs in order to succeed.

We mentioned earlier that these Leadership Moments come in a variety of sizes. So, learning to recognize them is key. But what do they look like in real life? And how do you know when one of them is staring you in the eyes?

Small leadership opportunities come along frequently. They are often found in the daily interactions we have with team members, co-workers, or peers. They are generally not a big deal in the overall scope of things — the opportunity to be fully present when someone is talking with us, the opportunity to make eye contact with a team member instead of looking at the phone or completing an email.

It is these small things that often matter the most, because they serve as a form of glue or contact cement for the relationships a leader has with team members. Why is this important? Because this is the very characteristic that binds workers together in the pursuit of a common goal. Without it, team members or departments have no real reason to support each other.

What do medium-sized Leadership Opportunities look like? They will typically impact a larger number of people or they will be of greater importance to the department or organization.

For example, a recent change in company policy has resulted in a series of operational changes for the team. It isn't a huge shift, but it does take some of the more senior staff members out of their comfort zones and requires them to perform a set of tasks in a different way. This isn't mission-critical, but it can be disruptive. How does the leader manage the discontent of these staff members?

Clearly, there are a number of different ways to handle a situation such as this. The important thing is that the leader recognizes that this has the potential to create larger problems if it is not handled effectively. The resolution will likely impact employee engagement, employee satisfaction, and overall productivity. Handled well and all three of these go up. Handled poorly, or not handled at all, and one or more of them is likely to drop.

An effective leader is conscious enough to see the longer term implications of a situation like this. With this consciousness comes a recognition that letting it drag on is not a good option. And it may also come with a recognition that addressing conflict can be uncomfortable and difficult, especially when it is with people we know well.

Large-scale Leadership Moments don't come along all that often. But when they do, everyone knows they are important. The scope of these opportunities tends to be very inclusive, impacting entire teams, departments, even organizations. What is not always so clear is the role the leader will play in it.

This is the heart of **The Leadership Nexus**. Leaders not only need to understand what they bring to their jobs — they also must understand what their jobs demand of them. It is in these large opportunities that this recognition of the needs of the position emerge most clearly. What is important here is that leaders understand what these demands entail while also recognizing what skills they need in order to ensure success.

An example of one of these large-scale opportunities is the event we detailed at the beginning of this book. The internet goes out in a remote location, threatening the ability to get work done for everyone at the facility. The leaders involved in resolving the situation each needed to understand their separate roles, the roles of their teams, and the needs of their individual clients.

Failing in this resolution means a significant loss of revenue, client respect, and future business. But, as we saw earlier, it is possible to resolve the situation and still fail to lead effectively. A win-lose solution (resolve the internet problem, but perpetuate a system in which the wrong people are solving it) will manage the short-term problem. But it can also unintentionally lead to a recurrence and it will not teach the individuals involved (both team members and customers) who should most appropriately be involved in the solution.

A win-win solution (which this team eventually employed) resolves both the short-term outage problem and the long-term communication and empowerment issues. In this case, the Managers learned how to step forward as soon as they discover a problem, work with their Director to ensure the most effective solution, and then go to work handling it. In the meantime, the Director communicated up the chain of command how the problem will be solved, who will be solving it, and what the time frame will likely be. The higher level leaders then communicate to their worried counterparts what is being done and reaffirm their confidence in both the solution and the individuals implementing it. **Win-win**.

In general, it isn't necessary for a good leader to spot every one of these Leadership Moments. It **IS** important to be alert and to recognize enough of these moments to impact the team and the organization in the most positive direction possible.

In short, it is WHAT a leader does with these moments that determines his/her effectiveness. Effective Leadership Moments are characterized by a conscious set of thoughts that trigger a deliberate set of actions.

Practicing the ability to recognize and act on **Leadership Moments** is a characteristic of a growing, developing leader. We know that changing everyday thought processes has a direct impact on performance. Try keeping track of your work day thoughts and see what you would like to change. Given that a normal human being has somewhere around 6,000 thoughts per day, there are plenty of opportunities to take advantage of even a small percentage of them.

Practicing new behaviors can lead to the discovery of a new sense of accomplishment as skills improve. This is what leads to a substantive change. Getting more comfortable with an improved ability to act out of a higher level of leadership makes it easier to think the thoughts that higher level leaders think.

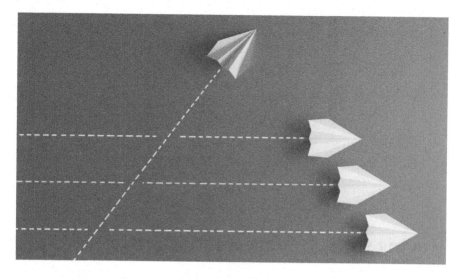

CHAPTER 8

Moving to Another Level

> *"Average leaders raise the bar on themselves;*
> *good leaders raise the bar for others; great leaders*
> *inspire others to raise their own bar."*
> Orrin Woodward

How do you move from one of the five levels to the next? By thinking about and doing the things that leaders on those levels think about and do. In this section we would like to put forth some suggestions that you can look at and practice. Doing this will help you move from your current leadership level toward your ideal.

Moving from Transactional to Managerial

Preparing for a move to level 2 lies in recognizing the importance of teamwork and understanding how to help others work better together.

- Look for opportunities to work in larger, more diverse teams.
- Offer more suggestions on how the team can perform its routine tasks more effectively.
- Volunteer to participate on new or existing committees.
- Practice surfacing potential conflicts and learn how to resolve them.
- Learn more about how effective teamwork can positively affect work processes.

Moving from Managerial to Tactical

- Look for opportunities to examine existing policies and procedures.
- Ask for more leadership opportunities, both inside and outside of the department.
- Expand committee participation to include areas outside of your primary expertise.
- Create opportunities to talk about longer-term strategies with your one-up.
- Ask for permission to initiate a new project.
- Look for opportunities to strengthen your creative abilities, both personally and professionally.
- Expand your reading to include books and articles on strategic thinking and risk-taking.

Moving from Tactical to Strategic

- Seek opportunities to participate in projects outside of your area of expertise.
- Look for individuals in other areas of the organization with whom you can develop new and stronger relationships.
- Ask for leadership opportunities that stretch your abilities and

put you into contact with other parts of the organization.

- Set aside time to look at strategy development unencumbered by your daily tasks.

- Find someone inside the organization who can guide you and teach you about the higher-level relationships and operations that occur outside of your vision.

- When you are pulled into the weeds, get out of them as quickly as possible and then ask for updates.

Moving from Strategic to Transformational

- Read as much as possible about anything and everything. Expand your internal boundaries and stretch them farther than you think they can go.

- Look for interesting people outside of your industry and learn what is happening in their worlds.

- Practice expanding your imagination by intentionally putting yourself in uncomfortable situations.

- Embrace the unknown.

- Talk with innovators in other industries to learn how their industries could impact yours.

- Get involved in forward-thinking organizations that challenge your existing view of the world.

Create a workspace where you can identify the areas of change that you will commit to working on over the next several months. As you successfully achieve the first ones, move on to the others.

Remember that the goal is to use your natural skills to the best of your ability. Add to them by practicing the skills necessary for success in your current role and for advancement to the level of leadership that you desire.

Using All 5 Levels

The qualities and characteristics that accompany each of the levels we have described are fundamental elements of success. And, as we have seen, each level is unique in its need for these qualities. What is important is the balance between them, the amount of time you, as a leader, dedicate to them.

What we are suggesting here is that success at an individual level requires an appropriate blend of the skills and abilities of each of the five levels. A Transactional leader should have some understanding of the greater strategic direction of the organization. It is perfectly okay, even desirable, for a Managerial leader to bring some degree of creativity and broader thinking into interactions with staff members.

Think about a truly transformational leader, an individual who is in the process of dramatically and fundamentally changing an industry. Should this individual occasionally get onto the floor to see what is happening in real time? Of course! The insights from this type of interaction are essential for a deep understanding of how the new processes are actually working.

Are these forays onto the floor a mistake? Did they make the Transformational leader less effective? No to both of those questions. What they do is enable the leader to maintain a connection with the workers and with the products. But they don't remain on the floor long enough to create role confusion among the staff. Nor do they keep this leader from his or her primary responsibility — creating amazing new products.

Each leader must find a way of balancing their thoughts and actions in a way that is most effective for their role. Too much creativity and we can lose sight of the ground. Too much fire-fighting and we lose sight of the big picture. To function as an effective leader we must be willing to consistently re-examine the focus of our thought and action time; balancing them as the needs of the role require.

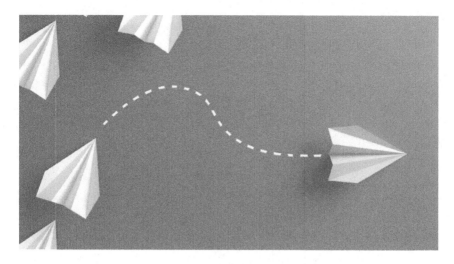

CHAPTER 9

Understanding
The Leadership Nexus Assessment

*"If you want to be comfortable — take an easy job.
If you aspire to leadership, take off your coat."*

Unknown

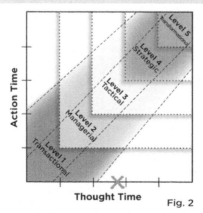

Fig. 2

Reading the results of **The Leadership Nexus** Assessment is pretty straightforward. It begins with finding your two axis scores. The horizontal axis of the model is the Thought Time score and is identified by an X (Fig 2). This score tracks the amount of time spent thinking and making decisions about a wide range of work issues. Scores toward the left indicate thoughts that are focused more upon daily routine and situations that need immediate attention. Scores at the right of the scale indicate thoughts that are more global or strategic.

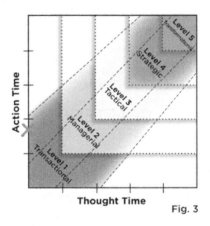

Fig. 3

The X on the vertical axis (Fig 3) is the Action Time score. This score indicates the amount of time spent on a wide range of work tasks in a typical day. Scores toward the bottom end indicate work time that is spent on regular routine, emergencies, and basic personnel issues. Scores toward the upper end indicate time spent on strategy, evaluations of process, and efforts to change the nature of the organization's work.

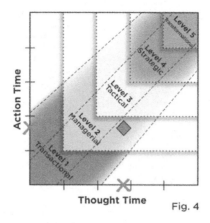

Fig. 4

The diamond found inside the model (Fig. 4) represents the intersection of Thought Time and Action Time, **The Leadership Nexus**. This score indicates the alignment of thoughts, decisions and actions.

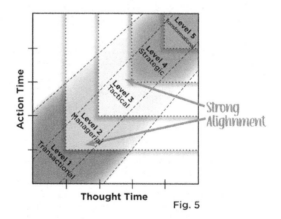

Fig. 5

The areas of solid color in the model (Fig. 5) represent areas of alignment that are fairly strong and consistent. A score within these areas means that the individual's thoughts and actions are aligned to a high degree. The more solid the color, the more closely aligned the scores.

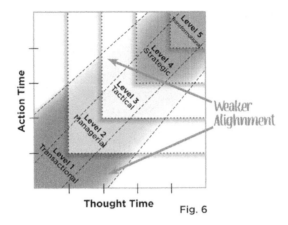

Fig. 6

The areas of moderate or fading color between the dotted lines (Fig. 6) represent scores that are less than aligned. This indicates the individual's scores in either Thought or Action are higher in one than they are in the other. And why is this a problem? Because it often reflects a periodic loss of focus, an increased amount of stress, and/or an individual who struggles occasionally, or who misses details in carrying out a leader's directives.

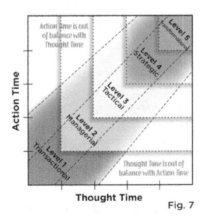

Fig. 7

A composite score (Fig. 7) that lands in the white area of the lower right of the model reflects a leader who is spending considerably more time thinking about strategy but is spending less time acting on it. The risk in this lack of alignment is that it can cause the leader to look like a dreamer without a solid grounding in how to get things done.

A composite score that lands in the white area of the upper left of the model reflects a leader who is spending more time performing higher level activities, but not expending the thought time necessary to make them effective. The leader's risk in this case is that he can become detached from a strategic focus and unable to connect actions with a vision of the future.

Struggling to work at their highest levels is a client complaint that we often hear. In **The Leadership Nexus**, this struggle shows up as a diamond in a level that falls below their actual role or position. For example, a manager or director finds their score in the Transactional level, or a vice-president finds their score in the Tactical level instead of the Strategic level. Seeing a graphic representation of this operational reality can present them with a language with which to understand what they are feeling as well as ideas on how to change it.

Why is alignment important?

The Leadership Nexus looks at the alignment of Thought Time and Action Time. But why is this important? So what if my thoughts are ahead of my actions? Why does it matter if my actions are ahead of my thoughts?

Thought Time, the measure of the time spent thinking about things during the workday, reflects a leader's focus. Realize it or not, this focus indicates an internal set of priorities. The most effective leaders want to be thinking about the things that are most relevant to the role they play.

Action Time is much the same. What an individual acts on reflects their priorities. "Actions speak louder than words" is both real and true. What a leader spends time on matters.

Thought Time Ahead of Action Time

The goal in **The Leadership Nexus** is to match Thought Time with Action Time in the areas most critical to the leader's role. But what happens when a leader's thoughts are ahead of their actions? One possibility is that the leader is out of step with their actions and has trouble grounding thoughts in reality. This is the hallmark of ineffective production. Another possibility is that the leader is stuck in a reality that is both unsatisfying and frustrating — hamstrung by circumstances (budget, staffing, and lack of training) in a way that practically ensures dissatisfying results.

Action Time Ahead of Thought Time

What does it look like when a leader's Action Time is outpacing Thought Time? Picture a leader who is taking his team into arenas that have not been adequately thought through. The idea sounds great, but suddenly the team is beset by customers, clients, or team members unhappy with the new direction because it doesn't meet their needs or unacceptably upsets their existing processes. What looked like a great idea suddenly turns into disaster.

We see this form of misalignment with coaches/leaders who report themselves as too deep or too often in the weeds, unable to spend significant amounts of time on the things they feel are the most satisfying and the most fun. Over time this leads to a sense of burnout and unhappiness that can destroy creativity and production.

This is why alignment is important. Making sure that what we do lines up with our ability to think it through, and that our actions are actually grounded in a set of well-thought-out ideas.

Misalignment in either direction can be hazardous to a leader's health and career. The best leaders find a healthy balance between these two worlds: the world of thought and the world of action. And they do this effectively within the context of the role they are required to play.

CHAPTER 10

Where do I go from here?

*"Go as far as you can see; when you get there,
you'll be able to see farther."*

J.P. Morgan

What we have tried to do in these pages is to look at leadership from the inside out. Rather than identifying abilities or qualities that leaders can bring to their companies, we have laid out an approach that focuses on aligning thoughts and actions with the skills and characteristics that are needed for success at each level of an organization.

If you have seen enough here to whet your appetite for a more in-depth look, click on the link at the end of the book and take **The Leadership Nexus** Assessment. When you receive your results workbook, begin the journey of learning how you can more effectively bring your particular skills to your position and discover how to align them with the needs of the level in which you are working.

In the process, remember the four basic principles of **The Leadership Nexus** we talked about at the beginning:

- **Effective leaders use their minds differently as they grow** in experience and insight. They develop a more sophisticated ability to use logic and reason as well as emotions to consider possible responses to difficult situations. They use their accumulated wisdom to make decisions that will help them, their team members, and their organizations create successful solutions for complex problems.

- **Effective leaders learn how to act in a way that is aligned with their thoughts and decisions.** They formulate visions of where they want to go and then they expend the proper amount of energy to get there.

- Effective leaders think and act in ways that are aligned with the needs of the roles for which they are hired. Since each organizational level is different, the leadership needs are different as well.

- **Effective leaders recognize leadership opportunities when they appear.** We call these opportunities Leadership Moments. An outstanding leader knows how to spot them and how to act on them effectively.

We are at a time of transition throughout the world. Great transition calls for equally effective leaders. Our goal, and our hope, is to help further the development of a generation of great leaders. We trust that you will find **The Leadership Nexus** to be an important step in your personal journey to greatness.

We wish you many leadership moments.

SPECIAL OFFER

With this purchase of **The Leadership Nexus** book, you are entitled to a ***FREE short version report of The Leadership Nexus Assessment™.*** This report will provide you with a basic understanding of your score and where it fits in **The Leadership Nexus** levels.

For a more detailed description of your score and an in-depth examination of how you can use your results to improve your leadership skills, consider upgrading to the full report available on **The Leadership Nexus website. (TheLeadershipNexus.com)**.

To access the assessment:

FOR EBOOK PURCHASERS

You will need to enter the Amazon Order Code you received when you purchased the ebook on Amazon \. To locate it:

- Go to your Amazon Account.
- Click on "Your Orders".
- Locate The Leadership Nexus™ order.
- In the gray box that offers the Order Details, highlight and copy the "Order #."
- Go to **TheLeadershipNexus.com/Get-My-Code** on our website.
- Complete the required information, and paste your Amazon Order Code in the designated box.
- You will be sent a code to access the The Leadership Nexus Assessment.

FOR PAPERBACK BOOK PURCHASERS

- Visit **TheLeadershipNexus.com/Get-My-Code** on our website. Once you complete the form, enter the code **LEADNEX100711**, and click submit. You will automatically be sent a code to access The Leadership Nexus Assessment.

Thank you for your interest in **The Leadership Nexus**™.

Made in the USA
Monee, IL
26 October 2020

45601504R10039